WELCOME TO
DINNER,
CHURCH

WELCOME TO
DINNER,
CHURCH

Verlon Fosner

 Seedbed

Printed in the United States of America

Cover design by Strange Last Name

Page design by PerfecType

Fosner, Verlon.
  Welcome to dinner, church / Verlon Fosner. – Frankin,
Tennessee : Seedbed Publishing, ©2017.

      102 ; 17 cm.

      ISBN 9781628244205 (paperback : alk. paper)
      ISBN 9781628244212 (Mobi)
      ISBN 9781628244229 (ePub)
      ISBN 9781628244236 (uPDF)
      ISBN 9781628244607 (DVD)

      1. Evangelistic work--United States. 2. Church
      renewal--United States. 3. Church. 4. Pastoral
      theology. 5. Westminster Community Church
      (Shoreline, Wash.) I. Title.

BV3790 .F676 2017   269/.2   2017934041

SEEDBED PUBLISHING
Franklin, Tennessee
Seedbed.com

This book is dedicated to the leaders and congregation of the ninety-three-year-old church that unashamedly reached for a new day with me. They proved to be more motivated to reach the lost neighborhoods in our city than to retain the comfort of their cherished way of doing church. In my opinion, they are the boldest church in America.

CONTENTS

INTRODUCTION

Christianity is the greatest rescue project the world has ever seen. And yet the vast majority of churches across America have become ineffective at evangelism and slipped into decline. The percentage of Americans who hold to a secular worldview now outnumbers those who hold to a Christian worldview.

There are reasons to be hopeful, however. The life of Jesus is still a welcomed talking point, even among staunch seculars. While their interest in church attendance is low, their interest in talking about Christ and the things he has brought to the world is high. Some believers lament that America is no longer interested in Christianity. That is not true. We do, however, have a sociological problem: our traditional way of doing church does not fit the majority of secular people. It is time to reexamine our ways of doing church if we want the unchurched to go to Jesus with us.

It was against this backdrop that our then eighty-five-year-old Seattle church started to test numerous new approaches for our neighbors. After many failures, the Lord opened our eyes to the way the first Christians did church—around dinner tables. As we began to employ the Jesus dinner table theology, our church began to thrive in pointing unchurched people toward the Savior. And soon, we were thriving in every other way too.

This introductory book is designed to reveal some mile markers on the dinner church path and to help Christians know how to work effectively with Jesus at one of his dinner tables. Further, this book is designed in such a way as to be discussed in a group setting. While many know how to be fruitful churchgoers in a traditional church, most have never considered how to effectively serve in an apostolic era church.

For a group to learn this approach to church, it will require some meditation, some permission giving, some prayer, and a new look at some old scriptures. To get the most out of this material, I recommend each group approach each of the following chapters in five repeating ways:

READ the assigned chapter before attending the discussion.

WRITE an answer to each of the discussion questions at the end of each chapter.

ATTEND the group discussion that has been scheduled by the leadership team.

WATCH a short video that will be played at the beginning of each session.

DISCUSS your answers, observations, and questions from the reading and videos.

Whether you use the book as a group discussion resource in the above suggested manner or read it as a personal overview of the dinner church vision, you will gain insight into one of the most dynamic and compelling strategies available to the church today.

It is my hope that you will feel the heartbeat of the Jesus dinner table, which has been extraordinarily effective at rescuing the lost throughout Christian history. I welcome you into the joy of taking many new people to heaven with you and your church!

1

REBIRTH

It was a Seattle summer evening as my wife, Melodee, and I walked home to our apartment. We had just finished the sixth week of our dinner church in that neighborhood, and already the room was filling up with more sinners, strangers, and seculars than our historic church had seen in years. Our eighty-five-year-old church had gone into serious decline in recent years, and though we had been several hundred people strong at one point, we were now shrinking so fast that we would likely be closing our doors in a few short years. Surprisingly, that fact did not discourage our people; rather, it motivated us to find a new way of doing church that would resonate with our neighbors.

So, we began to test new approaches to church, all of which were very different from our history. While this was an exciting time for our leaders, one test after another ended in failure. Our Christians enjoyed the new gatherings we were testing, but each of them failed to gather lost people and turn them toward the Savior. Soon, our season of innovation began to show signs of exhaustion. It was at this point we started to hear a still, small voice beckoning us to look back, *way* back, and try doing church as the early apostles did—around dinner tables. It seemed unlikely to us that such an ancient way of doing church would resonate with a cosmopolitan city like Seattle, but we had nothing to lose; we were already great at failure. So, with a go-for-it attitude, we launched a dinner church. But this time, things were different. The room started to fill up with unchurched people, and there was an unexplainable divine spark that started to flow into the room. Rich and poor, sinner and saint, dark skin and light skin all sat together, ate together, laughed together, and started to talk about Jesus. It was beautiful to watch.

And this brings us back to that walk home with my wife on that Seattle summer night after our sixth dinner church gathering. I was holding her hand when I heard the words come out of my mouth: "Honey, I think we have just seen our future." Those words would prove to change our lives—and our church—forever!

Secularism

Christianity is a rescue endeavor. However, in recent decades many American churches have drifted away from the rescue mission and have become teaching events, worship events, and gatherings of Christian friends. These approaches to church have left their congregants detached from evangelism and confused as to how they are supposed to live out the Great Commission to reach the lost. This is especially true as secularism has increased in our land to the point that a chasm has developed between the churched and the unchurched. The idea of believers engaging in spiritual conversations with their neighbors and coworkers has become increasingly difficult. Common ground is becoming harder to find between those with a Judeo-Christian worldview and those with a secular worldview. Yet, many church leaders still hold the hope that their congregants will initiate compelling conversations of faith with their secular neighbors to the point that one day they will accept an invitation to come to church. Sadly, this hope is seldom rewarded. There are a few gifted evangelists in our churches that can make this form of soul winning happen, but most people cannot.

Eras of the Church

To better understand our situation, a simple overview of church history is helpful. The first three hundred years of Christianity were known as the apostolic era. During this time Christians used the "Jesus dinner table" approach to church, in which gatherings occurred at dinnertime, included the stranger and the poor, and preached the stories of Christ. The next season of the church started in the fourth century and is referred to as the Christendom era. During this season of church history, Christians employed the "sacred space and liturgy" approach to church, in which sanctuaries of grandeur were constructed, enabling people to feel God's presence and be drawn to him. For the past five hundred years, the church has been living in the Reformation era, and the central feature of church gatherings has been the teaching of the Scriptures in a presentation format to develop believers in Christian spirituality. While this five-hundred-year-old form of church was never strong in evangelism, it is the approach that most defines the present-day church.

The Middle- and Upper-Class Church

One of the stark differences between the apostolic era churches and the next two eras is the shift in the socioeconomic assumptions. Roman historical documents from the early centuries chronicle how the vast majority of Christians were lower-class slaves, laundry workers, and individuals of lesser social stature. This was not a surprise to the people of that day because it was in line with the people Jesus lifted; he unapologetically reached for the poor and the broken first, and instructed his followers to do the same. But when Rome centralized Christianity as the state church, they started constructing buildings equal to the government palaces to be worthy of the people of stature. And the church has never been the same since.

The theological idea of preferring the poor has fallen on hard times in the mainstream church to this very day. An honest review of American churches reveals that we are located mostly in middle- and upper-class neighborhoods. Further, our buildings and programs assume that those in attendance already have their survival needs met. Abraham Maslow made a great contribution to society when he published a graph titled "Hierarchy of Needs."* Maslow's graph revealed strata of human need, with the ones at the bottom being survivalistic in nature (the need for food, shelter, safety) and the ones at the top being fulfillment-oriented in nature (the need to love and be loved, the need for self-actualization). To evaluate Christian gatherings, it is obvious that the upper-strata needs are the only ones being served, not the lower-level survivalistic needs. This is perhaps the greatest difference of the dinner churches; they clearly focus on the basic needs of a human being first.

---

*See https://en.wikipedia.org/wiki/Maslow%27s_hierarchy
_of_needs#/media/File:MaslowsHierarchyOfNeeds.svg.

Ineffective in Evangelism

Church leaders are now consistently reporting that their traditional Sunday-morning churches are no longer reaching their unchurched neighbors. The idea of going to an exclusive religious campus to study Scripture with an exclusive circle of religious people does not fit the desires or the sociologies of seculars. While the Sunday-morning experience may fit people who have had church attendance in their family line, it does not fit those whose families have never attended church. Such is the situation of seculars; traditional Sunday church does not fit their sociology. With seculars now outnumbering Judeos in almost every zip code across the nation, this sociological misalignment is starting to leave a mark. We are now closing eighty churches a week across our land. This closure rate is the result of many years of ineffective evangelism. The fact is that only one church out of a hundred is growing from the conversion of lost people. It is little wonder why most Christians have given up on evangelism and settled into a life of church attendance and occasional volunteerism in their church programs. Further, it has been so long since the rescue mission has been practiced as a whole church effort, most Christians have forgotten it was supposed to be the primary expression of their church.

There Is Hope

However, hope is on the horizon. New breeds of Christian leaders are beginning to work on new ways of doing church, and these fresh expressions of the church are showing great promise in reaching lost populations that would never attend a Sunday proclamation gathering. These new approaches are built around clear redemption plans, focus on a particular lost people group, and are done in a way that believers can easily find a role in the evangelism effort. Any group bold enough to stop doing church the way they want and start doing a church for a particular circle of lost people soon discovers that evangelism becomes easy again.

This is where the dinner church shines; it is very effective at doing church for sinners, strangers, seculars, and the poor in a way that they see and feel Jesus. Dinner church is a Great

Commission environment that makes evangelism natural and easy. Accordingly, there is a new dinner church opening almost every week somewhere across the country. We are now witnessing a rebirth of the two-thousand-year-old approach to church—the Jesus dinner table.

DISCUSSION QUESTIONS

1. What is your favorite memory of church?
2. What is your greatest memory of a lost person coming to Christ at your church?
3. Have you ever been involved in leading someone to Christ as a part of your church's efforts? If so, how did it happen?
4. What would you need from your church for you to become effective at evangelism?
5. Do you think most of your neighbors would accept an invitation to attend church with you? If they did come, do you think they would come a second time? Why or why not?
6. Do you agree that the church's primary mission is the rescue of the lost? Why or why not?

THE FIRST DINNER CHURCH

The first church was very different from what we do today. While there are many blessed occurrences in any church that gathers in Christ's name, there is value in reconsidering the way the first church functioned that arose in the immediate shadow of the life, death, and resurrection of Jesus.

Jesus' Dinner Table Theology

The first church was very serious about the dinner table theology that Jesus left them. Many Christians today read Scripture through the assumptions of the Reformation era in which we presently live. Accordingly, they overlook the centrality of the dinner table in the life of Jesus, which ultimately inspired the vision of church that sprang up in the book of Acts, and the vision of church that expanded to the Gentiles. Jesus used the dinner table profoundly throughout his ministry. In fact, many of the parables were told at his evening dinner gatherings, in which publicans and Pharisees alike were present. Whether it was the miraculous feeding of the large crowds, the dinners at Matthew's house with his sinner friends, the dinner at Zacchaeus's house, or the meal with the men on the road to Emmaus who recognized Jesus by the way he broke the bread, Jesus used the dinner table to reveal himself and embrace people into the kingdom of God. It is little wonder that the first versions of the church assumed the dinner table as the time and place to gather, because it was there that they expected Jesus to be with them in spirit in the same manner he had been with them in body during the years he walked the earth.

The Last Supper

Jesus did something at the Last Supper that further propelled the church toward the dinner table. It was here that Jesus actually verbalized a vision of doing church to his disciples. The historical backdrop of that evening is what gave such a clarion call for Jesus' followers to use the dinner table for the new church. It was the annual Passover in which Jewish people celebrated Israel's rescue from Egypt. Strangers were to be included, their impoverished and enslaved condition was to be remembered, the sacrificial lamb was to be consumed, and their miraculous freedom was to be celebrated. This was an entire dinner that had the themes of rescue, inclusion of strangers, inclusion of the poor, remembrance of the lamb, and the expectation of miraculous intervention. It was against this backdrop that Jesus told his disciples to turn the annual Passover dinner into a common event. That is the Jesus dinner table theology in a nutshell: gather the saint and the sinner, eat together, talk about Jesus, and expect divine interventions to show up.

A Dinner Church Is Born

It must have been a very compelling vision for the disciples, because immediately after

Jesus' ascension, the leaders went to work establishing these dinner gatherings together throughout their cities. In fact, it is a challenge to find any Christian gathering in Scripture that did not occur around a full meal. This was by design—Christ's design. The book of Acts is filled with people gathered around food, with the poor and the stranger, talking about Jesus, and experiencing one divine intervention after another. The dinner church is seen in a deeper way in the book of Mark, which is actually Peter's preaching recorded by John Mark in his mother's upstairs room at what was probably the first church in Jerusalem. They would eat dinner together and, afterward, listen to Peter preach. And what would Peter preach? The stories of Christ.

Dinner Church for the Gentiles

When Paul took the gospel to the Gentiles, he used the form that fit their culture best: large feasts. In fact, they were called agape feasts, or love feasts. They would eat together, include the poor and the stranger, and remember Jesus together. This helps us understand 1 Corinthians 11:20–22, where Paul was rebuking the church for hoarding their food and excluding the poor. He charged them for not being a good representation of the way the body of Christ should function (i.e., not discerning the body of Christ). While some have used this verse to protect the symbols of Communion or Eucharist, the dinner church context makes it clear that Paul was redirecting the Corinthians back to the truth that including the poor in the meal was the Jesus way. Understanding the dinner church backdrop also helps us understand the book of Jude, which was to be sent around to the churches in that region, and assumed that all of them were dinner table churches that functioned in the likeness of the Last Supper.

What Happened to the Dinner Table Church?

The church that flowed into the second century continued to hold the understanding that it was the dinner table where Jesus would continue to meet with sinners and saints alike as they gathered in his name. Just as Adam and Eve had a place and time when they walked with God in the cool of the day, the first church understood that Jesus would meet them at the dinner table, eat with them, and intervene in their lives. The Jesus dinner table served as a divine portal between heaven and earth for the early church. It was not until the fourth century that the dinner church theology became stifled and started to fade from the understanding of the Christ-followers. In fact, it took until AD 682 at the Council of Trullian for the last vestiges of the agape churches to be stamped out from the life of Christian church.

The Great Table Waiting for Us

There are a couple of beautiful tables offered to us as some of the final images in Scripture. In Revelation 3:20 we see the image of Jesus knocking on the heart's door, and if a person opens that door, Jesus will come in, sit at the dinner table with them, and eat with them. It is the great desire of our Lord to be with the people of this world in a very close way, and to accomplish this closeness he invokes the imagery of a dinner table. Then in Revelation 19:9 we are told there is coming a day when God will raise up the church to meet Jesus the Bridegroom.

And what is the setting for this long-awaited reunion? The greatest feast in all of history—the marriage supper of the Lamb.

Resurgence of the Jesus Dinner Table

The absence of the Jesus dinner table has had significant negative impact upon the evangelism effectiveness of the church. During the first three hundred years of Christianity, the population of the church grew to more than twenty million among deeply diverse and pagan cultures. I cannot help but note that this remarkable growth occurred while the church was deeply influenced by the Jesus dinner table theology and functioned as a dinner church.

I also note that we are once again among diverse and secular cultures. If the Jesus dinner table was indeed a place and time when the Lord would meet with sinners and saints alike, then it was the place where the divine invitation of Christ could be most easily heard by the wayward heart. This is a rich heritage of the church that is again needed today.

I am stirred to the point of tears every time I think of how deeply the sinners of my day need to hear the divine invitation from Christ himself in their own hearts. Historically and scripturally, that divine invitation has been the loudest when the church gathered lost people to their tables, talked about Jesus, and let him knock on their hearts' doors. "Oh Lord, bring a resurgence of your dinner table and your divine invites to our world today! And may your church regain a vision of your dinner table again!" This is my daily prayer.

——————— DISCUSSION QUESTIONS ———————

1. Why do you think most Christians do not see from Scripture how much Jesus used the dinner table?

2. How has the scripture about the Last Supper changed you?

3. Can you imagine Jesus not leaving a pattern of gathering for his church? Why or why not?

4. What does it say to you that the Acts churches and the Gentile churches met around Jesus tables?

5. How do you think the church would have been different if it had never reduced the full meal to a couple of Communion symbols?

6. What does it say to you that the reunion event after we are gathered to heaven is the greatest banquet table of all time?

EARLY CHRISTIAN MIND-SETS

The dinner church is a two-thousand-year-old approach to Christian gatherings. Any group desiring to do church this way needs to consider what the first-century church valued and how they thought. The Reformation era in which we live has shaped our Christian mind-sets in ways that are far different from how the first church functioned. To state it clearly, the dinner church does not align with the present-day Christian any more than our way of doing church would be valued by a first-century Christian.

Too Much Truth

It was a Tuesday night in Seattle, eleven years ago, when thirty of our leaders sat in stunned silence. We were meeting once a week to discuss what to do about our declining church. But on this night, our college pastor called out the elephant in the room, and we were all uncomfortable with what he'd said; the whole group sat quietly looking around the room at each other.

The evening began with the discussion of how our neighbors would know Jesus if he lived at our church's address. Everyone drew from Jesus' actions in the Gospels and put together an image of what he'd probably be doing for our neighbors. But then came the weighty follow-up question: How do our neighbors know us? This is where our college pastor interjected, "They don't know us. All we ever do is go back and forth to this church building."

That was our first brush with just how different we were from the ways of Jesus, and it was too much truth for us to handle. But after our emotions settled a bit, that statement became a necessary splinter in our souls that drove us to change our version of Christianity, and our version of doing church.

The God-Family Rescue Business

The primary mind-set of the first-century church was rescue. In fact, the gospel was explained in terms of rescue for the first one thousand years of Christian history. While this idea has slipped away in recent centuries in favor of explaining the gospel as a justification from sin and the church being seen as a Christian purity system, the early church felt they were a significant part of the greatest rescue project the world had ever experienced. They called Jesus the Savior of the world and recognized that his coming here proved that the God-family was in the rescue business. Jesus' stories in Luke 15 of the lost coin, the lost son, and the shepherd leaving the ninety-nine behind to go rescue the lost sheep all played very loudly in their souls. Jesus was in the rescue business, and so was the physical body he left here on earth—his church. Therefore, his church would need to rescue people as directly as Jesus' activities and dinners had rescued people when he was on earth.

Replicating the Works of Christ

Another mind-set of the first church was their commitment to repeat the works of Christ as expression of their Christianity. When Jesus was on the earth, he only did a few things with his time, but he repeated them over and over again. He spent some time in prayer, he performed healings and miracles, he spent large amounts of his time with the poor and the broken, he rebuked judgmental people because they frustrated sinners from coming to God, he spoke often about the kingdom of God breaking into the affairs of earth, and he taught his disciples to replicate his works. These were the repeating works of Christ that are clearly visible in the Gospels, and each of them was very effective in establishing the rescue business upon the earth.

Some of the words Jesus left as he approached the end of his time on earth make it clear that his followers would be better at doing his works than even he was (see John 14:12). Thus, he handed off a list of behaviors for his followers to continue; his life was a template for us to do our lives in similar ways and usher the rescue interventions of heaven into the lives of people. When the first followers were called Christians, it was because they were doing the same works as their Master. Their Christianity was not about propagating a doctrine as much as it was replicating works of Christ in their daily schedules. Their goal of discipleship was not to memorize the values of Christianity; it was to develop behavioral Christlikeness. He healed people, so they healed people; he spent time with the poor, so they spent time with the poor; he ushered the kingdom of God into people's lives, so they ushered the kingdom into people's lives; and he rescued people around dinner tables, so they did as well.

Theologian John Crossan observed that if we were to watch Jesus when he walked the earth, we'd mostly see him healing and eating.* What an interesting two-point mission statement for a church: healing the broken and eating with the sinner.

---

*Graydon Snyder, Julian Hills, and Richard Gardner, *Common Life in the Early Church* (Harrisburg, PA: Trinity Press International, 1998), 141.

Sent-ness

Another mind-set of the early church that has dropped off the radar is the idea of "sent-ness." The first Christians expected to be sent to a lost people to rescue them in the likeness of Jesus. Sometimes they were sent by the Spirit to go down the Roman road system to another village, town, or even a major city. By the days of Paul, it is estimated that as many as forty thousand Jews had felt called to move to Rome with the intent of rescue.* Though they were scared into silence by the depravity of the Roman culture and had to be called back into action by Paul in the book of Romans, the idea of sent-ness was an obvious heartbeat of the early church.

Citywide-ness

Similar to sent-ness was the early church's understanding of "citywide-ness." Christians were not always sent away; often they were sent to a nearby circle of lost people in their own city.

---

*F. F. Bruce, *Apostle of the Heart Set Free* (Cambridge UK: Paternoster Press, 1977), 380.

The Jerusalem Christians were the first ones to go from one under-gospeled neighborhood to the next until they had filled the entire city with their stories of Jesus. They did not locate at one address and call whosoever will to come to them; rather, they entered the next social circle closest to them and found a way to include them at a Jesus table.

Paul watched the same thing occur in the large Hellenistic cities throughout the Roman realm. In fact, their agape feast churches spread through the urban cities with such effect that the term "pagan," which initially meant country-dweller, came to mean "unchristian." This was because if you were from the city, you'd know all about the Christian message, but if you were a pagan, you probably did not.

This urban saturation occurred because Christians felt sent from one neighborhood to the next until there were agape Jesus tables everywhere serving different circles of lost people. Many church historians believe that the reason Constantine adopted Christianity as the state church wasn't so much because of his conversion, but because the Roman world had become a Christian world.

New Christian Identity—New Way of Doing Church

Once a group admits how different their version of Christianity is from the first template of Christ-followers, they can let some of the early church mind-sets seep into their hearts. Soon, go-to-church versions of Christianity start to wane, and a missionary identity starts to emerge. Also, the idea of doing gatherings solely for believers stops making sense, and a desire to do church for sinners starts to rise.

Our Seattle group realized that our method of church had been flowing from our version of Christianity. Once we accepted the missionary identity, we then needed a lost people to rescue and a vision of how to do church for them. We were aching to create a Great Commission environment and engage in the works of Christ. Once those desires started bubbling in our souls, the dinner church vision came alive in our imaginations. In short, once we had adopted the mind-sets of the first-century Christians, their version of church needed to be adopted as well. We needed the Jesus dinner table church, as much as the Jesus dinner table church needed us.

Healing for Churches

Jesus left behind some great instruction for any of his churches that are declining. He did this in the parable of the great feast found in Luke 14:15–24. In this story the king invited his nobles and honored rulers, but they refused to come because they were mad at him. So, he instructed his servants to go out and invite the subjects and commoners. But when his banquet hall was still unfilled, he ordered his servants to invite the poor, the disenfranchised, and even the homeless that lived along the hedge-rows, until the house was full. The point of this parable is so simple most miss it: if your church is empty, drop down on the socioeconomic ladder and invite the poor and the broken until your ministry house is full. Restoring a declining church is actually quite a simple fix—get your eyes on a new circle of people who know they need help and start including them at your ministry tables. Sadly, most declining churches have never applied this parable to their ministry.

Many churches are dying today because they do not feel sent to any lost circle of people.

And if they did feel sent to a nearby lost neighborhood, they would not know how to include them in the gospel. Recovering the early Christian mind-sets and their Jesus dinner table theology completely healed our church, and gave us a far greater future than we had ever experienced in our past. I have a sense that this same healing is on the divine agenda for many other stalled churches across our land.

─────── DISCUSSION QUESTIONS ───────

1. Do you believe that the God-family sees themselves as being in the rescue business? Why or why not?

2. Why is it so difficult for churches to admit that they are ineffective at evangelism?

3. Do you and your church need to feel a greater urgency to take sinners to heaven? Explain.

4. Do you think most Christians believe that it is their calling to replicate the actual works of Christ that he exhibited when he was on earth? Why or why not?

5. Do you or your church feel sent to a particular circle of lost people? If so, whom?

6. What do you think would occur in most stalled churches if they felt called to do church for a nearby specific circle of sinners?

4

THE NEIGHBORHOOD
FAMILY TABLE

I was driving a few blocks south of our church campus one day when, suddenly, I became unusually aware of my surroundings. Have you ever had the experience where things seemed to shift into slow motion for you? This was like that. But, after driving a few more blocks, the feeling went away. Over the next few weeks, every time I drove that direction, the same thing would happen. Finally, one day, I just pulled over to the curb and asked the Lord what was happening. What I did not know then was that I was experiencing a Macedonian call. Much like in Acts 16:9, when Paul had a vision of a Macedonian man waving for him to come, I was hearing a Seattle neighborhood call for me to come to them; the Spirit was drawing us toward an under-gospeled people in a particular neighborhood. Now, after having planted a dinner church in that neighborhood and being drawn into seven more under-gospeled neighborhoods, I can unequivocally state that Macedonian calls still happen!

Sore Neighborhoods

After seeing our ability to fill up dinner church rooms in several locations, I assumed it was an urban answer for the church, and even published an academic paper to that end. However, soon other dinner churches sprang up in small towns and became just as effective as we had been. I had to retract my first assessment and acknowledge that dinner churches tend to thrive in any sore neighborhood in any size town.

We all understand that there are middle-class and upper-class locations in our towns, but most leaders have not embraced the fact that the lower third of the population also exists in every town. The lower third do not earn enough to pay their bills, and their lives are full of struggle. Fox News reported in 2013 that two out of five American families are now relying on food banks.* That means that more than a third of the population live at unsustainable levels.

Another large group of the American population that church leaders tend to overlook are the second-life singles. These are individuals who have already ruined one life and are trying not to ruin another one. They have an ex-spouse and kids who hate them; are living in a small, run-down apartment; are working at a meaningless job; and are just hoping that they can stay away from the bottle this time. These are the ones who live alone, but wish they didn't. They are perhaps the most isolated individuals in society, even more than the poor. The Scriptures refer to these people as strangers (see Matthew 25:31–46), and they are located in hidden pockets throughout every town. These are the isolated people of our communities.

Where do the poor and the strangers live? They live in poor neighborhoods that are scattered throughout every town in America. Theoretically, one out of every three neighborhoods is a sore neighborhood. Most middle- and upper-class

---

*Bill O'Reilly, *The O' Reilly Show,* Fox News, April 2013.

people do not realize how close the lower third actually are to them. After all, the poor don't shop in the nice boutiques on Main Street, and they don't attend most of our nice churches either.

Those Who Already Know They Need Help

For churches to overlook this struggling population is a departure from our Lord's ways. He gave preferential treatment to the poor without apology; not because they were more important, but because they had greater need. In Mark 2:17, Jesus said that he did not come to those who were healthy, but to those who knew they needed a physician. How interesting that Jesus looked for people who already knew their lives weren't working well.

I fear that most churches are hoping to attract people who have not come to awareness that they need the intervention of the Savior, even though Jesus targeted the ones who were in need and already knew it. Undoubtedly, Jesus would target the sore neighborhoods if he were here. And yet an honest review of American Christianity is that we have located most of our churches in middle- and upper-class neighborhoods.

While the traditional church tends to do well with people who earn enough to live comfortably, the dinner church embraces the rest of the American population. And that is a large percentage of our towns. In fact, there is likely a struggling neighborhood within a few blocks of almost every church in America, whose residents would never consider going into a church building on a Sunday morning, but they would welcome a dinner church in their neighborhood.

One Block off Main Street

Sore neighborhoods are usually noticeable once a group starts looking for them. They usually have a large percentage of lower-rent apartments; run-down cars; broken windows; graffiti; and older, single people hanging around the sidewalks. But, sometimes, the bleakness is difficult to see because it is tucked one block behind a nice boulevard. Seattle has a dinner church in one neighborhood where the main street is lined with hundreds of beautiful, $3,000-per-month apartments and condominiums. And yet, our dinner church fills up every night with people who could never afford those units. Where do they come from? They live one block back in run-down houses, old apartments hidden behind old-growth trees, and in vans parked along the curbs. What looks at first glance like a great Seattle neighborhood filled with hipsters is actually a poor neighborhood.

Doing Church for the Sore Population

To be called into a sore neighborhood is to be called to the financially challenged and the lonely. These are the under-gospeled people circles that know they need help. What a mission field for the church, if we could only open our eyes to see a Macedonian vision waving us to them! These are the people who find it difficult to sit through one of our Sunday-morning gatherings, stand to sing songs, sit through announcements and offerings, and listen to a sermon for thirty minutes because they have a churning in their stomachs from worrying about how they are going to feed their children their next meal or make rent the next day.

Our presentation versions of church do not fit their sociological realities, but a dinner church does. There, they are welcomed to a dinner table, where they eat perhaps the best meal of their week, get treated like valued family members, laugh, hear the words of Jesus, and are prayed over. Now, that is something that fits their lives' realities.

The Power of Abundance

There is surprising power in a buffet table that is loaded with an abundance of food. This is especially true for the financially challenged and the lonely, as access to good, hot food actually breathes security and a feeling of worth into their souls. But beyond that, it opens up their hearts to the divine invitation of Christ. An abundant feast that is paid for by Christ reveals an abundant gospel. One of the most overlooked parts of Jesus feeding the five thousand and the subsequent feeding of the four thousand is the baskets of food that were left over. Those large baskets of leftovers reveal a message of divine abundance. People who know their lives are not fully supplied need to see abundance. And when the Jesus table shows them abundance, they begin to understand the generosity of God and feel valued. The spiritual concepts of an attentive God and unfailing love become believable once they see examples of abundance, if even from a dinner table that Jesus and his people have paid for. Homeless meals serve just enough, but these are not homeless meals; they are Jesus dinner tables, and they are abundant.

The Big Event in the Neighborhood

Very few significant events happen in sore neighborhoods, primarily because the people who live there cannot afford it. This is a great opportunity for the church. It is a significant event to put on a weekly feast with abundant food, artists painting metaphors of the Gospels, musicians singing the great songs of the church, and preachers telling soul-stirring stories from the life of Christ and then praying for favor and healing to descend into the room. A neighborhood dinner table provided by Christ's people should expect to see an increase of peace in the streets, a decrease in crime, and interventions of the Lord in the lives of the people who live there. Dinner churches change entire neighborhoods.

DISCUSSION QUESTIONS

1. Have you or your church stopped to consider how many people in your town do not earn enough to live there without help? Why or why not?

2. Do you know where the sore neighborhoods are in your town? Where?

3. How does it affect you to know that Jesus only pursued the people who already knew they needed help?

4. Why does the image of abundance make such a difference for the gospel?

5. How does it make you feel that the version of church you enjoy isn't the version of church that will help most of the lost people in your town feel Jesus?

6. How is a dinner church different from an outreach?

TALKING TO
SECULARS

When we began our first dinner church, we
had some fears about doing life with seculars.
Only 5 percent of Seattle attends church, and
another 5 percent used to attend church. That
means 90 percent of our city holds to a secular
worldview, making us the most unchurched
city in the nation. The knowledge that Seattle
is so well versed in their secular values made
us feel we were entering into a den of Christian
opposition; that turned out to be untrue. We put
out little tent signs on each table explaining
that there would be a Christ-story and a prayer
at the end for anyone who wanted to stay. Our
fear was that people would eat and run before
that portion of the evening gathering. Our even

deeper fear was that our Christ-stories would spark reaction and argumentation. And our deepest fear of all was that once people realized we were doing a Christ table, they would never come back, and we would have empty rooms after a few months. Wrong, wrong, and wrong.

Christianity, Yes; Churchianity, No

The crowd started to grow immediately, they made it a weekly habit to be there, and they did not walk out during the Christ-story. After a few months, they started engaging in the Christ dialogue in some way. Sometimes their interest was revealed in a follow-up question about something that was preached, or by asking what the sermon was going to be about at the beginning of the evening, or even by taking jabs at pastors for preaching so long (with a twinkle in their eye). But the next week they were right back with us—eating, laughing, high-fiving, and jabbing.

To our surprise, we learned that Seattle was not against Christianity; it was "churchianity" they did not like. Churches that met on Sundays to talk, but seldom helped out with obvious social needs, and then held judgmental attitudes toward anyone of a different lifestyle all culminated into a distasteful thing for seculars. And yet, they were mesmerized by the person of Jesus and enjoyed talking about him and the good he has poured upon the earth.

The seculars' interest in Jesus is good news for our church. Talking about Jesus is the only thing we need to do to be a vibrant voice for the Lord, and they were good with that. After all, the gospel is Jesus, not a religious purity system. As soon as our Seattle guests realized that our dinner tables were not an outreach that was subtly trying to drag them over to a Sunday-morning church somewhere, they relaxed and started talking about Jesus.

The Divine Invitation

Paul made it clear that he preached Jesus and him crucified (1 Corinthians 1:23). When you think of it, the only thing the apostles had to preach on was the life of Jesus. They had no notion that their letters to each other would one day be bound together with the Gospels as a holy book. To them, those were just letters, but the life of Christ was the living Word of God, and that is what they preached. In Romans 10:17, Paul stated that faith was birthed when people heard about the Word of God, which they interpreted as the life of Christ. To them the Word wasn't a book; it was a life—Christ's life! So, as they preached the stories of Christ, faith was birthed in the hearts of the sinners. With this in mind, it is little wonder why it is so hard for us and our teaching-centered churches to get faith to birth in sinners' hearts, because we are so focused on information and trying to affect their belief system. The apostles, however, just told the stories of Christ because they had the confidence that in so doing a divine invitation from Christ himself would start to echo in the hearts of sinners. While our Seattle seculars might not be interested in doctrinal debates, their hearts are open to the stories of Christ. That insight was a game-changer for us.

Comfortable Table Talk

The strength of a dinner church is how easy conversations can occur at the table. While there is preaching and prayer from the pastor, the greatest opportunity for Jesus to call to the souls of our guests lies in the table talk the remainder of the hour. The only problem is, most Christians are only used to talking to other Christians about anything deeper than the weather or football. The knowledge that talking about Jesus is a welcomed thing among seculars should be helpful to any group wanting to reach the lost. There remains an obvious difference in the value systems, however, between seculars and Judeos. The longer someone has been ingrained in the church world, the more he or she will have to learn and unlearn some things.

No Christian Trump Cards

Something most groups will have to unlearn is their tendency to play their Christian trump cards. While I will talk about this at greater length in a later chapter, many will need to come to terms with the fact that they are accustomed to a right/wrong explanation of the Scriptures, while seculars hold to a worldview that has no absolutes. Some Christians have railed against this as though Christianity will collapse if they cannot speak with absolutes. But when Jesus is at the center of the conversation, his presence serves as an undeniable absolute, and if that was a good enough starting point for the apostles when they faced the Gentile population, why would it not be a good enough starting point for us with the New Gentiles that live in our cities? There is scriptural precedent for laying down the right/wrong trump cards and, instead, trusting the Savior to be good at his job—even if we are not defending the line between sinner and saint with every breath (see Galatians 3:23–26).

A Repeating Pattern of Conversation

Something most people will need to learn is to let lost people take the lead in the conversation and steer how deep they want to go. After hundreds of hours of table talk in Seattle, we noted that almost every conversation with our new friends followed a similar outline: life, limitations, and spirituality.

Talking about Life

Like an onion skin, the outer layer of conversation is almost always about people's lives: jobs, family, hobbies, jokes, to-do lists, and interesting things they've done in their past. While guests are talking on this level, it is time to listen to their life stories, laugh when things are funny, and be sober when things are serious. It is also key for each of us to share things about our lives in a back-and-forth way. Inviting them into our lives is as important as them inviting us into theirs.

Talking about Limitation

After a while, most guests will shift the conversation to the deeper onion skin layer of limitations. It is at this point that they begin to speak of something in their lives that is not going well. Maybe they feel limited because of a lack of money, lack of friends, frustration with family relations, struggles in finding jobs, inability to quit being angry at someone, or inability to control their intake of alcohol. It is a great honor to be trusted with a new friend's frustrations and limitations; treat it as a holy thing to be invited to this level.

Many Christians must learn to practice some great discipline at this level and *not* start giving spiritual answers. Instead, now is the time to share some of our limitations with emotional honesty and, again, in a back-and-forth manner.

Most Christians assume that sinners feel guilt, and come to God for forgiveness. While this is true for some because of an egregious act they have done to someone else, typically seculars make their way toward the spiritual level because of limitation, not because of guilt. Guilt requires some polishing of one's conscience through spiritual teaching, which is something most seculars have made no time for.

So, when a secular invites us into their limitations, they are inviting us into a very deep place, and they are not far from touching Jesus. This is a big turn in the conversation, and should be respected.

Talking about Spirituality

Finally, a guest might invite us into the deepest onion skin level of conversation, which is spirituality. While this might be veiled at first, they might begin sharing some soulish answer they have investigated to address their limitation. Remember: people are driven into spiritual depths because of their limitations, so they are looking for answers to explain their lives and alleviate their frustrations. They might start talking about Buddhism, mythology, drowning their frustration with drugs or alcohol, sexual distractions, religious studies, meditation, and so on.

At this point, we, again, have to practice some restraint, and let them talk freely about their spiritualities. Further, we must be interested and inquisitive about how they approach their spirituality and how well it is working for them. Then finally, after all of that, we are able to share a bit of our spirituality—which, of course, is Jesus. This is not a time to upstage or correct their spirituality; it is a time to share our most meaningful Christ-stories and encounters. But keep it brief and quickly turn the conversation back to their spiritual investigations, so as to maintain the back-and-forth conversation format.

Once a spiritual conversation has begun, the last thing we want is a well-meaning believer pulling out a trump card or doing a hostile takeover of the conversation. If that happens, our guests' journey toward Christ will be undercut, and they won't trust us again with the deeper regions of their soul.

Let Them Shift the Conversation

Not long ago, a man walked up to me and asked me to sit by him that night at dinner so we could talk about Christianity. I was surprised. I had sat next to this man probably twenty times over the past few years, and the deepest we ever got was that he liked to drink, and was always waiting for his next paycheck so he could buy more alcohol. But that night, for some reason, he was ready to shift the conversation directly into the spiritual arena. I am sure the many conversations we'd had about his life and mine, commingled with the stories about Christ and the prayers, had led him to open up the deepest level of his soul—and in a blunt way at that. And did we ever talk about Christ that night! After much discussion about what Jesus might say to him if he were to ask, I left him with a prayer to pray. He said he would, and I am still waiting to hear how his conversation with Jesus went. But after several years, suddenly Jesus was on the docket.

Talking to a secular about life, then about limitations, then about various spiritualities, all the while letting them be the ones to shift the conversation, is a very rewarding part of the dinner church experience. It is great when Christians have learned to relax and enjoy the new friends that the Lord has given them. Then one day, without warning, they will find themselves talking comfortably about Jesus with a dinner friend. And, of course, it will be a comfortable conversation, because they were invited to be there.

——————— **DISCUSSION QUESTIONS** ———————

1. How does it make you feel that people with secular worldviews outnumber people with Judeo worldviews in our country?

2. Do you agree that the primary pushback from seculars is not Christianity, but churchianity? Why or why not?

3. Do you think most Christians feel that it is their job to change a lost person's belief system to be effective in evangelism? Explain.

4. How does it make you feel that evangelism is primarily friend building, and the rest will come naturally at a Jesus table?

5. Why do you think most experienced Christians pull out scriptural trump cards when someone talks about sinful activities?

6. What do you think would be the result if most Christians honored the natural outline of conversation: (1) talking about life, (2) talking about limitations, and, finally, (3) talking about spirituality?

PRAYING FOR BROKEN PEOPLE

There has been a long association between Jesus the Healer and Jesus the Savior. It began even before Jesus' life on this earth, in Isaiah 53, where it was predicted that he would be wounded to cleanse our sins and that by his stripes we would be healed. It takes a particularly clever theology to allow Jesus to be our Savior without expecting him to breathe healing upon us too.

Healed First

Looking at healing through a research lens reveals that many people who come to Christ receive healing first. This is especially true in Africa, where almost 100 percent of the people who come to Christ do so after they or someone in their family has experienced healing. In Asia, almost one-third of salvations experience healing before their conversion. Only Western civilization has experienced a diminished association between Jesus the Savior and Jesus the Healer, with less than 3 percent experiencing healing prior to experiencing the Savior.*

The answer for this discrepancy might be as simple as prosperity. Western Europe and North America have enjoyed such wealth, with subsequent health care, that people in these regions are not as desperate for healing as the nations in the global South. Gatherings of world theologians have formally noted that the American church, in particular, is far more affected by our prosperity than we realize, and thus we have underdeveloped theologies of poverty, suffering, and healing.

The dinner church is a Great Commission environment that draws many broken people into its rooms. Could anyone keep Jesus the Healer away from such a place as this? Despite

---

*David Lim, "Holy Spirit in the Church" (lecture, Christian Resource Institute, Kissimmee, FL, July 25, 2010).

our North American citizenship, the need for healing is high, but the desire of the Healer is higher. Those who feel called to serve at one of his dinner table churches might want to consider their role in introducing Jesus the Healer as much as they'd consider introducing Jesus the Savior to their new friends.

Simple Healing Prayers

The first step in praying for broken people is to realize that healing is one of the works of Christ that he asked his people to replicate. Revealing himself as the Healer is his idea, not yours. Thus, flowing through one of your simple healing prayers is what he likes doing. He only asks us to pray for people when the opportunity presents itself.

My wife, Melodee, had a sweet, quiet lady come to her a few months ago because she sensed that Melodee was in need of prayer. My wife said, "Well, yes, in fact, I need a healing touch from the Lord." So, this quiet-mannered woman softly prayed for Melodee, and instantly my wife knew something divine had occurred in her and she was healed.

Over the next few weeks we couldn't stop talking about the gentle way this lady had approached Melodee. What an example of a simple healing prayer offered quietly and unnoticeably in a noisy room!

Socially Appropriate

A second step in praying for healing is to eliminate the picture of a TV healing evangelist as the template for healing prayer. I cannot think of a single time when Jesus offered healing to someone by praying as some of the people on TV do. In fact, I can't think of an instance when he even raised his voice. He maintained the social norm of communication for the place and time where he was engaged in healing. This is important to remember: you do not have to become socially awkward to breathe healing into someone.

At dinner tables some things are socially appropriate, and some things are not. However well-meaning some might be, to gather a bunch of Christians around someone sitting at a table and pray loudly in spiritual and authoritative ways is not culturally normal for dinner tables. It is awkward, embarrassing, and something Jesus wouldn't do. So, take a page out of the Jesus book and don't do it. While elders' prayers and loud spiritual prayers may be the pattern of some churches, it is not a pattern to be broad-brushed across environments where sinners and seculars are present. Paul warned the Corinthian church not to promote such spiritual prayer when sinners were present that it would make them say, "You guys are crazy," but rather, maintain a socially acceptable tone that would make them say, "God is surely among you" (see 1 Corinthians 14:23–25).

Jesus' healing prayers and Paul's words serve as handrails for us when it comes to praying for seculars. A form of prayer that is socially acceptable in a dinner room is the quiet, one-on-one prayer. It will usually be very appreciated and helpful to listen to someone share a need of brokenness, feel a prompt in your heart to pray the prayer of healing, ask the individual if you could pray for him or her, and then offer a quiet prayer that doesn't embarrass your guest and that others at the table don't even know you are doing. Favor will flow into that person, the Healer will show up, and divine intervention in some form will start to stir. This is the gospel we have in our hands—that God's favor, healing, and interventions are available to us all.

Healing Is Not an Event

Another step we need to take if we are going to pray for healing is to know what the goal of our prayer is. Many Christians view healing as an event in which someone prays, and then a healing immediately removes the ailment as a divine occurrence. While that certainly does happen from time to time, that is not the actual goal of praying the healing prayer. The actual goal is to invite Jesus the Healer to come into someone's situation, start walking with that person, and start affecting healing in a daily way from that point forward. Healing is not an event; it is a walking relationship with the Healer. The prayer of healing is what releases the Healer to start walking with and intervening in a person's brokenness. We are doing Jesus and the person we are praying for a disservice if we only acknowledge the instantaneous healing event, since the Healer most often works in daily and progressive ways.

More Healing Virtue than Most Realize

Some months ago, I saw one of our dinner church regulars in a coffee shop. I sat near him and we started to talk. He told me that he was frustrated at one of his friends for not even trying to kick heroin. He went on to tell me that he had kicked it last year, and if he could do it, his friend should at least try.

I was intrigued by his recovery story, so I asked him how he did it. He looked at me with a baffled look on his face, and then he pointed at me and said, "You guys did it." I asked how we did it, because none of us even knew he had a heroin problem.

He then explained that the heroin voice always went away when he was in our dinner church room. And whenever that voice came back, he knew that all he had to do was make it until 5 p.m., because we had a dinner church every night of the week somewhere in town. When he walked into the room, ate a great dinner, laughed with someone, heard a story about Jesus, and listened to another Jesus prayer, that heroin voice would be gone for another few days. He concluded by saying, "After three months, the voice went away altogether and hasn't been back." Think of it: this man found healing, and we did not do anything.

It reminds me of the woman who had been sick for twelve years. When Jesus came to her town, she slipped behind him and touched the hem of his robe. He turned around and asked who had just been healed, because he had felt healing virtue flow from him. Of course, the woman presented herself, but note that she was healed and Jesus did not even know he was doing it (see Matthew 9:20–22). There is more healing virtue in a dinner church room than most realize. The emphasis need not be on the volume of our prayer; instead, just cooperate with the healing virtue that is already flowing, because Jesus is present at his table, and his healing is present with him.

Let the Healer Out

I have a pastor friend from Singapore who tells his church at the end of every gathering, "Remember who you are. Now, go out and heal someone, and I'll see you next Sunday." That makes me smile, because it so reveals an awareness of the healing Jesus who lives within us. We have invited Jesus to live within us, but when do we let him out? Once we decide to let him out, he is going to come out as he really is—sometimes as Savior, sometimes as Provider, sometimes as Comforter, and sometimes as Healer.

———— DISCUSSION QUESTIONS ————

1. How does it affect you to know that healing plays such a significant role in the majority of conversions around our world?

2. Why don't you think the American church offers the Healer as much as we offer the Savior?

3. Do you think most Christians see healing as an event rather than a walking relationship with the Healer? Why or why not?

4. Do you believe there is more healing virtue at work than most Christians realize? Explain.

5. Can you see how there might be more healing virtue in a dinner church than in other forms of church? Why or why not?

6. What would happen if the average Christian in America let Jesus out as much as they invited him in?

7. Could you ever offer a healing prayer for a broken person in a simple and quiet way? Why or why not?

THE PATH OF SALVATION

Dinner churches are Great Commission environments. They are special places, functioning differently than traditional churches, which are predominantly filled with Christians. Many believers and Christian leaders have been in the exclusive houses of faith for so long, they have forgotten what it is like to work in a Great Commission environment. If we are going to work effectively with Jesus in one of his dinner table churches, we are going to need to think like evangelists rather than churchgoers.

Leave the Weeds Alone

Jesus told a challenging parable about a farmer who planted some seed. The next morning there were weeds growing among the seedlings he had planted. His servants readied themselves to pull the weeds that day, but the farmer stopped them. "Don't pull the weeds; you'll also pull up the good plants if you try. You just nurture the good seed, and we will separate the crop from the weeds at harvesttime" (see Matthew 13:24–29).

What makes this story so challenging is that Jesus used this story to actually instruct his followers to ignore some of the works of the enemy in people's lives in favor of nurturing the gospel. Wow! That is vastly different from the way many church folks think! There is a stream in the body of Christ that feels they are not serving Christ well if they are not patrolling the border between sin and righteousness all the time with every person. They feel it would be poor Christianity to tolerate sin in someone's life, when it is the exact opposite that is true.

If we are going to be effective in one of Jesus' harvest fields, we are going to have to start working with people who have many wayward things at work in their life—too many to force them to a right/wrong line and to start fixing all at once. For this reason, Jesus focuses his people on watering the gospel that has been planted in people's lives and intentionally over-looking major issues of sin that exist. Spending the majority of our time around fellow Judeos has eclipsed the harvest priority and dulled our harvest skills. Most American Christians need to brush up on their understanding of the path of salvation for sinners, rather than assuming that the path for Judeos is a one-size-fits-all approach to Christ. Leading seculars to salvation is a case of leading them to Jesus down *their* path of conversion, not yours.

The Judeos Right/Wrong World

After the death of Jesus, the gospel began to spread into the Jewish populations. This Judeo gospel had a right/wrong assumption to it, which made perfect sense to a people who had a seven-hundred-year history with the law of Moses. Thus, the gospel for the Jews was presented as a law gospel. The people's conscience and behaviors had been so shaped by the law that they were at a place in their spiritual development to submit to the authority of God, acknowledge his moral code, and embrace Jesus as one who would empower them to stay within the curbs of the law.

A Different Path for the Gentiles

When Paul prepared the gospel for the Gentiles, he altered the path of salvation to fit a culture that had no history with a law from God. He reduced the law language and the authoritarian imagery of the kingdom of God, and replaced it with a grace gospel. The Gentiles, who were primarily the forefathers of democracy, saw kingdoms and singular authoritarian entities as primitive. So, to force them to bow their will before an authoritarian God that they barely believed in and immediately line their lives up to a moral code of God's choosing would be the equivalent of pulling up the gospel seeds with the weeds. Paul obviously believed that the gospel would be immediately rejected before it had a chance to prove its worth because of their egalitarian culture. So, in Galatians he started explaining the gospel as faith-to-faith, which was similar to the apostle John's explanation of grace-to-grace. This allowed the Gentiles to walk with Jesus in one chapter of their lives, then graduate to another chapter with the Lord, from one state of grace to another state of grace. This was critical to the salvation of the Gentiles, which the skilled apostles understood.

A Judeo Explanation in a Gentile World

We find ourselves at exactly the same place in our nation today. There is the church, which well understands the right/wrong approaches to the gospel because we are Judeos, and we have learned to trust God even though we have granted him authoritarian power over our lives. But we are called to rescue seculars, who are the New Gentiles, and are not ready to grant authoritarian status to God and align every area of their behaviors to a moral code as the entry price into Christianity. I am so glad that the church has been at this intersection before and left their notes throughout the Epistles, especially Galatians. Paul's grace-grace path simply taught the Gentiles of his day to walk with Jesus in a state of grace, then as Jesus bid them, to step forward into another state of grace, and another, until Christ was formed in them. Rather than imposing an immediate moral code upon unprepared people, he expected Jesus to be good at his job of being the Savior and to lead them step-to-step, faith-to-faith, strength-to-strength, and grace-to-grace (see Romans 1:17 and John 1:16). These are all phrases found throughout Scripture that speak of this kind of path of salvation. While Paul was comfortable to use law-like language when some in his day were trying to promote a license-gospel that attempted to use the freedoms of grace to create lewd and perverted versions of the gospel, he still ignored the law gospel in favor of the grace gospel when it came to the Gentiles. If Paul would offer that path of salvation for the Gentiles of his day, why wouldn't we offer that path for the New Gentiles of our day?

The Sinner's Prayer

Our dinner churches are filling up with New Gentiles. As wonderful as it is to be reaching people who would never come to a Sunday proclamation gathering, it is stressful for Christians who have been rooted in Judeo values to not force the seculars onto their path. It takes some meditation and divine permission-giving for many Christians to learn to feel comfortable offering a grace path to the sinners they meet at our tables. Without challenging their sin, we take them to Jesus; without insisting that they follow the pattern of confession of sins before Jesus saves them, we take them to Jesus; without forcing them to pray the Sinner's Prayer, which has only been around for 150 years, we just take them to Jesus. In so doing, we are in no way soft-selling the gospel, instead we are exercising great soul-winning skill.

Flowing with Generous Grace

In the 1500s, Jacobus Arminius starting speaking of prevenient grace. What he meant by this was the grace that Jesus poured upon people before they realized it was he that was doing it. Arminius referred to the grace people received after they came to see Jesus' work in their lives, and they began to cooperate with him in the grace he was already pouring into their lives, as concomitant grace, which means cooperative grace. For those who work with seculars, it becomes obvious that there is a huge world of grace working upon them, long before they know about Jesus. While the Judeo world tends to think that we must believe before we belong to the family of God, the Great Commission environments and dinner churches flip that order and start embracing sinners to belong before they even believe that Jesus is working in their lives. Thus, we demonstrate our skill at evangelism and our ability to work with the prevenient grace that is flowing into our dinner rooms every night.

A Church Full of Skilled Evangelists

If a Judeo church is going to work with Jesus in one of his harvest fields, then we must hear Jesus instruct us to ignore the weeds of sin in people's lives and, instead, nurture the gospel that is forming in these New Gentiles' hearts. We will learn to overlook these sins because, like Paul, we are becoming skilled evangelists. We will also learn to ignore the weeds because we truly believe that Jesus the Savior is really good at his job, and he can take these New Gentiles from one state of grace to the next one until they look as much like the Master as we do.

I invite my brothers and sisters in Christ to offer the grace-to-grace path to the dinner church guests. Please. Thus, we will turn up the volume of Jesus' divine invitation, and start welcoming many seculars into the family of God. What could be more beautiful than that?

——————— DISCUSSION QUESTIONS ———————

1. What do you think about Jesus' instruction to leave the weeds alone that might be growing in people's lives?
2. Do you see the right/wrong presentation of the gospel as the predominant explanation? Explain.
3. How do you think that Paul replaced the right/wrong explanation of the gospel when he started reaching out to the Gentiles?
4. Have you ever compared the seculars in America to the Gentiles that Paul reached with the gospel?
5. How does it affect you to hear that the Sinner's Prayer has only been used by the church for the last 150 years?
6. Can you see how inviting people to start walking with Jesus and trusting him to lead them toward his likeness in his time would be effective for seculars? Why or why not?

PRACTICAL ROLES

Holidays at the Fosners' are "chaordic." In other words, they are a perfect mixture of chaos and order. A large portion of each holiday seems to be lived in the kitchen. My wife and I, our three adult children, and their spouses and children, somehow squeeze into the fifteen-by-fifteen-foot kitchen. Hot pots of food are handed from person to person, assignments are called out in all directions, fingers are pointing out vacant counter space this way and that, and grandkids and granddogs are running through us, all down at knee level, on their way to the backyard. All the while, everyone is speaking over the noise in rapid-talk as they catch up on each other's lives while spooning out the mashed potatoes and pouring hollandaise sauce over the broccoli. Everyone is loud, everyone is busy, and everyone is laughing. It is a find-a-need-and-fill-it form of organization that has been perfected in our family over several decades. Finally, it is time to seat fifteen people plus tag alongs around a table that is far too huge for every other day of the year except this one, but on this day it's too small. Then we hold hands, thank Jesus for this big, hearty family, and eat the best meal of the year together. After we have eaten our fill, we often sit at that oversized table, talking, laughing, and sharing memories for a couple more hours. As I said, our family has become very accomplished at organized chaos.

Interestingly, dinner churches feel the same way, only bigger. There are twice as many people excited to see each other, working over huge pans of food, and talking over each other in the kitchen. There are ten times as many people gathered to eat their fill, pray to Jesus, and linger around the tables until "they kick us out of the community center!" Each night is another beautiful night of outward chaos that somehow instills a sense of inward order. Go figure! Even amid the chaordic atmosphere, there are still roles that need to be filled for these to become effective Great Commission environments.

Everyone Is an Evangelist

Engaging believers in evangelism is the most difficult thing for pastors to do. The idea of trying to verbally affect the belief system of a lost person seems overwhelming to most congregants. But what if evangelism was something an entire team did together? And what if it had nothing to do with trying to get someone to believe in Jesus but, instead, had everything to do with setting a big table for them to feel Jesus for themselves? Could that be evangelism? Yes, if it is a dinner church.

Whether a person is a cook, running a buffet table, painting on an easel, or setting up tables, everything one does while serving at a dinner church is evangelism. After all, most of the people who will fill up the room each night are sinners, strangers, and seculars. Even after many years, there is a constant flow of lost people who are seeing and hearing Jesus' knock on their hearts' doors. So, let me say this again clearly: if you are serving at a dinner church at any level, you are an evangelist!

Tithe unto Poverty

Dinner churches are one of the most inexpensive forms of church planting that is occurring today. Church leaders are continually shocked when I say that, but it is true. We rent community rooms by the hour, we use bi-vocational pastors, and a great feast can be provided for three dollars per plate. Thus, paying for a dinner church does not require grants or fund-raisers; rather, it just requires a few people who believe in God's age-old plan for lifting the poor: tithe unto poverty.

A simple study of Deuteronomy 12 and 14 reveals that one-third of the tithe was supposed to go into lifting the poor. When Jesus was on earth, he did nothing to disconnect the age-old plan; in fact, he even took note when a widow gave her last few coins to the poverty fund (see Luke 21:1–4). Proverbs 19:17 offers perhaps the most interesting insight by saying that when we help the poor, we are actually lending to God, and he will certainly repay his debt to us.

Wow! When it comes to giving to the poor, we are actually entering into a lending relationship with God! While this idea has fallen away from the church in recent centuries, the early church had a very clear understanding that God would repay them when they lifted the widows, orphans, infirmed, imprisoned, and the poor.

While we do put out an offering bucket at the head of the table so guests can engage in Christ's mission of lifting people, the majority of our income flows from believers who have recommitted to the tithe unto poverty. Let me again be clear: if you feel called to work with the Lord at one of his dinner table churches, he will need to borrow some of your money to pay for it. Please say yes. He will pay you back. He is good for it.

Samaritans

Each dinner church forms a core of people who feel called to that neighborhood to lift the guests that attend. Surprisingly, not all are Christians; at least, not at first. Jesus told the story about the good Samaritan to reveal that sometimes nonreligious people are more helpful than the religious ones. While I have found the Christians that are called to join a dinner church team to be very generous, I am constantly amazed by the number of Samaritans who join our core teams as well. God has woven into the fabric of humanity a desire to respond to need; if you fill up a room with broken and impoverished people, there will be a humanitarian response to it. These Samaritans are responding to that humanitarian impulse God placed in them. Interestingly, once there, they listen as hard to the Christ-stories as the guests do. And soon they see that Jesus is more like them than they ever realized. We sometimes feel that we are taking as many people to heaven that showed up to serve as to be served.

Find a Need and Fill It

Self-assigners enjoy the dinner church world the best. Anyone who is not good at finding a need and filling it should go to work on developing that skill right away, because that is the only organizational method that makes these Jesus table events flourish. It is amazing to me how each dinner church I've observed has found its unique way to self-organize. And if the personnel alignment shifts from one week to the next, the job still gets done, because everyone is finding needs and filling them.

Cooks and Culinary Teams

There are a variety of ways that people with culinary desires can find a meaningful role in a dinner church. Some of our dinner churches have a lead cook, others have rotating teams, and still others cook in a central kitchen and hot-box the food to the serving site. Whatever the case, the daily schedule is the same: they shop at noon, assemble to cook the food at 1:00 p.m., have the food ready for delivery to a truck or to a buffet table by 4 p.m., start serving at 5 p.m., box up all remaining food in to-go containers at 6:15 p.m. to send out the door in the hands of guests so there are no leftovers (this eliminates food storage needs and potential food-borne illness issues), and clean-up starts at 6:30 p.m. so that everyone is headed home by 7 p.m. That is the routine.

We recommend that every cook attain a food handler's permit that might be required by his or her state. This is inexpensive, easy, and usually available as an online certification. Note: a thirteen-week menu is provided in the dinner church handbook that is easy to prepare, great for big groups, relatively inexpensive, and yet creates an impressive and abundant feast.

Buffet Tables

Another role in a dinner church is buffet table service. The setup of this table needs to be impressive in color and in the organization of the food, and reveal obvious abundance. Chafing dishes create a catered look and are flanked by big salad bowls, bread baskets, and dessert platters. A lead buffet person has an important role, as he or she organizes the setup of the table, appoints food runners to keep the buffet table supplied, and oversees the many servers who will be coming and going throughout the evening. The servers on the line all use latex gloves, greet people by name as they come through, and treat people like family. Each server only works the table for a shift because they need to save time for the most important role in the room, that of the table friend (to be discussed later).

Musicians

Worship leaders and musicians in a dinner church have a significant role—of ushering the presence of Jesus into the room with their music. They are not trying to be relevant, they are not trying to showcase their skill, nor are they blending in secular cover songs that people might ask them to play. They are singing and playing the most reflective, reverent, and worshipful song sets that they would do on a Sunday morning in a worship gathering. Bringing in the presence of Jesus is one thing we can do for a sore neighborhood that others are not doing; our guests can find secular music in corner coffee shops and karaoke music at the local bar, but with us they "feel Jesus"! Our worship people sing throughout the entire dinner, except for when the preaching is occurring. While many seculars might not feel as comfortable singing worship songs as Judeos do, they will sit and cry while you sing the great worship songs of the church.

Artists

Many Christian artists have been frustrated because they have not known how to use their artistic talents for the gospel. They've got a job now! Setting a couple of easels up front with canvases (or hardboard palettes, which are cheaper), attaching top lights to draw attention to their work, painting a metaphor or an image that flows from the Gospels, working on the same painting for a few weeks if necessary, then sharing with the group what the painting says, is always a very meaningful component of a dinner church gathering. We call these "sermons on canvas." To watch a roomful of people study the developing canvas of a painter as they eat and hear them talking about the painting at their tables is a very interesting thing for the Lord to use in revealing himself to the souls of the onlookers.

Preaching

As stated earlier, preaching in the apostolic era was telling the stories of Christ's life and the stories that Christ told. With dinner churches being an apostolic church model, our preachers use the same speaking material as the apostles used. These are very simple, one-point messages that focus on one story from the life of Christ, and are followed by a short, soulish reflection on that story from the speaker, lasting an average of seven or eight minutes. There is an obvious absence of personal illustrations, jokes, exegesis, apologetics, and the other bevy of things that are usually included in Sunday-morning teachings. Martin Luther taught his young pastors that when it came to the Gospels, just read them and shut up. In other words, the simple stories of Christ have a way of soaking into the soul, and, there, the listener can actually hear the divine invitation of Christ.

A Friend of Strangers

Of all the roles already mentioned, befriending people is the greatest job in the room. Turning a stranger into a friend at a Jesus table is deeply Christlike. John Wesley realized this 150 years ago and moved Christians into London to create the Stranger's Friend Society. Their role was to sit around tables and turn strangers into friends. While you will often be sitting with people you've already turned into friends, it is a wonderful thing to always have a preferential eye for the stranger sitting alone.

The genius behind Jesus' call to befriend the stranger and the sinner is that friends have been following friends to salvation for two thousand years. The gospel has flowed down relational lines more freely than down any other human path. Jesus was called a friend of sinners, so we, too, will become a friend of sinners. When we turn a stranger or a sinner into a friend, we are opening up a very big door that over time will likely turn into a three-way conversation with Jesus.

Some of our dinner church team members are cooks, but they grab a plate and become a friend of strangers before the evening is over. Others are buffet table servers, but they grab a plate and become a friend of strangers before the evening is over. Still others are artists, preachers, or musicians, but they grab a plate and become a friend of strangers before the evening is over. Everyone eats! This is not an event where "we" serve "them"; rather, it is us welcoming them to eat at our tables with us and be our friends. This is the greatest happening in the room, and everyone turns strangers into friends at a Jesus table. Everyone!

——— DISCUSSION QUESTIONS ———

1. Do you believe that a dinner church environment would help you be an effective evangelist? Explain.
2. What do you think about the historic idea of "tithe unto poverty"?
3. How do you think most Christians would feel about including Samaritans on their dinner church's serve teams?
4. How do you think most church volunteers would respond to an instruction from a leader to "find a need and fill it"?
5. What roles in a dinner church would you most like to engage?
6. What growth needs to happen for you to become comfortable and effective at turning strangers into friends?

CONCLUSION

When Jesus came to earth as the Savior of the world, it was a demonstration that the family of God was in the rescue business. However, most of the American church has forgotten how to actually rescue lost people. We want to reach the lost, we talk about it often, we memorize the Roman Road, our pastors commission us to talk to our neighbors about Jesus, but the elephant in the room is that the vast majority of our churches are not getting lost people to Christ. And yet the person of Jesus is still popular in our land.

We have reached the point where it is time to consider finding ways of doing church that better fit the realities of our lost neighbors. This feat has been done before in the days of Paul, and it must be done again. To do so, we must wrestle with the following dilemma: Do we insist on continuing to do church the way we like, or are we willing to do a church for sinners and sore neighborhoods? That is a grievous thing to wrestle with. After all, most of us have holy memories of meeting with our church family and meeting the Lord at our Sunday-morning gatherings, and we just can't imagine that our lost neighbors will not see and hear Jesus in the church we have loved. But that is the truth. We cannot force our method of church upon them; it simply does not fit their sociology.

Some leaders today are investigating the question, When was the last time the church was effective in a reaching a secular environment? Church history reveals that when the church was holding tightly to the Jesus dinner table theology, sinners, strangers, pagans, and the poor were swept into the kingdom of God. This is undoubtedly why the first Evangelist, Jesus himself, embedded the gospel into the time and place of the dinner table. Any church or plant team that embraces that again will witness a divine spark come alive at their tables, and soon their rooms will fill up with more sinners than they have probably seen in years. There is something unexplainable that occurs when sinners and saints eat dinner together, talk about Jesus together, and witness the divine interventions of the Lord together. That is the dinner church, and it is beautiful.

It is my hope that you have you felt your pulse quicken at a few points during the reading and the discussion of this material. If this has happened, it is probably your heart's way of recognizing that the Lord is drawing you into a very interesting future.

It is now decision time. Martin Luther spoke of two conversions: the first conversion was to be drawn to the Savior, and the second conversion was to be sent back into the world with the gospel in our hands. This is one of those second conversion moments:

> There comes a day when we are asked to join the family rescue business. Is this that day for you?

> And there comes a day when we are sent by Jesus to a sore neighborhood. Is this that day for you?

And finally, there comes a day when we are asked to help raise up a dinner church. Is this that day for you?

What an honor to be invited to work with Jesus at one of his dinner tables! Your walk with Christ will never be the same.

APPENDIX
FOR DINNER CHURCH
DISCUSSION LEADERS

If you are a discussion leader for an upcoming dinner church start-up team, here are a few things that will help enrich your ability to get your participants ready to work with Jesus at one of his dinner table churches.

1. Order a copy of *Welcome to Dinner, Church* for each person who will be included in your discussion group. These can be ordered at: www.DinnerChurchCollective.net.

2. Read through the handbook so your field of information will be greater than that of your participants. This will assist your ability

to answer questions and get the group off of conversational sandbars when they occur. (And they will occur.)

3. Establish a nine-week discussion schedule. It is highly recommended that these be done in nine consecutive weeks, on the same evening of the week, and at the same place. (A routine time and place will enable the group to focus better.)

4. Give or send the *Welcome to Dinner, Church* booklet to each invitee, along with the scheduled time and place. Request that they read the introduction before coming to the first discussion meeting.

5. The night of the first discussion: (1) read aloud the five practices that are located in the introduction of the *Welcome to Dinner, Church* booklet; (2) show the "Introduction,"—the first of nine videos (the videos can be downloaded from www.DinnerChurchCollective.net or ordered on DVD); (3) entertain questions and comments; (4) lead a serious prayer that the Lord

will speak through this nine-week discussion; and (5) assign the group to read chapter 1 and answer the questions at the end before next week's meeting.

6. The night of sessions 2 through 8: (1) open in prayer; (2) play the corresponding video; (3) lead the group through the discussion questions, having them read their answers and leaving time for the group to respond to each other's answers; (4) give instructions at the end of the discussion to read the next chapter and answer questions before the next meeting; and (5) end with a concluding prayer.

7. The night of session 9: (1) open in prayer; (2) play the final video; (3) lead the group through the discussion questions, having them read their answers and leaving time for the group to respond to each other's answers, (4) have everyone take out their *Welcome to Dinner, Church* booklet and read the conclusion in unison; (5) lead a final prayer over your group that they officially join the family rescue business, commit to find their role in it, and say yes

to working with Jesus at one of his dinner table churches; (6) conclude by giving instructions on how you and the group are going to proceed from here with your dinner church plans (planning meetings? launch instructions? etc.).

ABOUT THE AUTHOR

Verlon and Melodee Fosner have led a multisite dinner church in Seattle, since 1999. In 2014 the Fosners founded the Dinner Church Collective, which is a church-planting network centered on Jesus' dinner church theology. In this decade, when more churches in the United States are declining than thriving, and when eighty churches a week are closing, Verlon and Melodee sensed that a different way of doing church was needed for their ninety-three-year-old Seattle congregation. It soon became obvious that they were not the only ones in need of a different path. There is a lot to be gained when church leaders begin to see open doors in the American landscape that they had previously overlooked. Therein lies the journey for those who will forge a new future for the American church.

The Fosners have three adult children, all of whom are married and bringing on the next generation, which for now means five grandchildren.

For more information go to
CommunityDinners.com
and
DinnerChurchCollective.net